Daddy's
Always Here
By Aaron Fields

Copyright © 2025 Aaron Fields. All rights reserved.

Published by The Write Perspective, LLC

All rights reserved. No part of this book shall be reproduced or transmitted in any form or by any means, electronic, mechanical, magnetic, photographic including photocopying, recording or by any information storage and retrieval system, without prior written permission of the publisher. No copyright liability is assumed with respect to the use of the information contained in this book. Even though every precaution has been taken in preparation for this book, the publisher/author assumes no responsibility for errors or omissions. Neither is any liability assumed for any damage that results from the use of the information in this book.

ISBN: 978-1-953962-737

 **There are many ways Dads can show up.**

He tells us stories of when he was our age. He says, "I've always wanted to be the kind of dad my future children will be proud of."

We find stories in the sky. Daddy says the clouds will carry our dreams.

Sometimes, we dance like the floor is lava and the music is magic. Daddy says, "joy is our birthright."

When we grow brave and walk ahead, Daddy still watches from behind. His love stretches far, even when his arms don't.

Even when Daddy feels sad, he never hides. He shows us that strength can cry too.

When we're nervous, Daddy kneels down and says, "You've already made me proud."

Each morning, Daddy walks me into a new day.

He says goodbye with courage in his voice. "Be brave. Be kind. Be you."

At night, we wrap up in stories that feel like hugs.

We listen, we learn, and we love. Daddy says, "Family is our forever."

When we cry, Daddy holds space. He says, "Your feelings are safe with me."

"I see you, Daddy whispers. "Let it out."

Even when he works hard outside, Daddy comes home to what matters most.

"Let's figure it out together," Daddy says.
Because learning is love too.

We talk about those we miss. Daddy says, "Love never disappears----- it echoes."

We pass peas, memories, and laughter around the table.

**Wherever we go, Daddy's love walks with us.
Because Daddy's always here.**

www.ingramcontent.com/pod-product-compliance
Lightning Source LLC
Chambersburg PA
CBHW041432040426
42450CB00022B/3475